I am
Simone Biles

BRAD MELTZER

illustrated by Christopher Eliopoulos

 ROCKY POND BOOKS

I am **Simone Biles.**

As a little kid growing up in Columbus, Ohio, I learned one of life's great lessons:

Family isn't just something you're born with.

It's something you build.

When I was three years old, my mother couldn't take care of us, so we were placed into a temporary home called foster care.

On the ride there, none of us said a word.

I was so anxious—it was scary to go live with a new family.

Our foster parents quickly realized I didn't like to sit still.

I was always running, jumping, cartwheeling, and climbing up high, especially to get lollipops.

HOW ON EARTH DID YOU GET UP THERE?

I'M A REALLY GOOD CLIMBER.

On the swing set, I was fearless.

I'd copy my brother and do backflips.

YOU CAN FLY, SIMONE!

When my grandparents heard that we were in foster care, they quickly came to get us.

It taught me another great lesson: You always take care of your family.

My grandparents raised me, guided me, and have always loved me.

The best part of our new house was what I saw in the backyard.

I ran as fast as my little legs would carry me.

For hours, I jumped and flipped,
my braids flying so high.

When I got back inside, the first thing my grandma did was wash and untangle my hair.

It might sound simple, but to have someone take care of me ...

To have her comb my hair as I daydreamed about this new life ...

My anxiety—the dread and fear I carried around—was gone.

I finally felt calm.

I felt like a princess. But most important, I felt all her love.

THERE YOU GO.

THAT'S MY GIRL.

When I was six, my younger sister and I were officially adopted by my grandparents.

In my room, I was so excited, I kept hopping around.

Back upstairs, I flopped onto my bed.

I was finally—and forever—home.

I wasn't the easiest to take care of.

In case you couldn't tell, I was always moving.

I'd swing on the slats of our bunk beds

or test how fast I could climb up onto my brother's shoulders.

THREE SECONDS, NOT BAD.

Then came the day my life changed.
I went on a field trip to a local tumbling gym.

A teacher there saw me doing backflips, so I came home with a letter inviting me to join the gym.

For a bundle of energy who couldn't sit still . . .

Gymnastics was just what I needed.

Even at six years old, I was muscular and strong.

WE WANT YOU TO CLIMB THIS ROPE USING JUST YOUR ARMS, WITH YOUR LEGS STRAIGHT OUT.

YOU PROBABLY WON'T GET FAR, BUT—

I got all the way to the top.

UM, SIMONE...

COME DOWN NOW...

PLEASE!

Another coach noticed how strong I was, using just my hands to lift my body.

SIX-YEAR-OLDS SHOULDN'T BE ABLE TO DO THAT.

AIMEE BOORMAN

SHE'S THE ONE I WAS TELLING YOU ABOUT.

Today, people say I'm a natural, as if it all came easily.
But I'll never forget learning to do a *giant*, which is a vital skill.

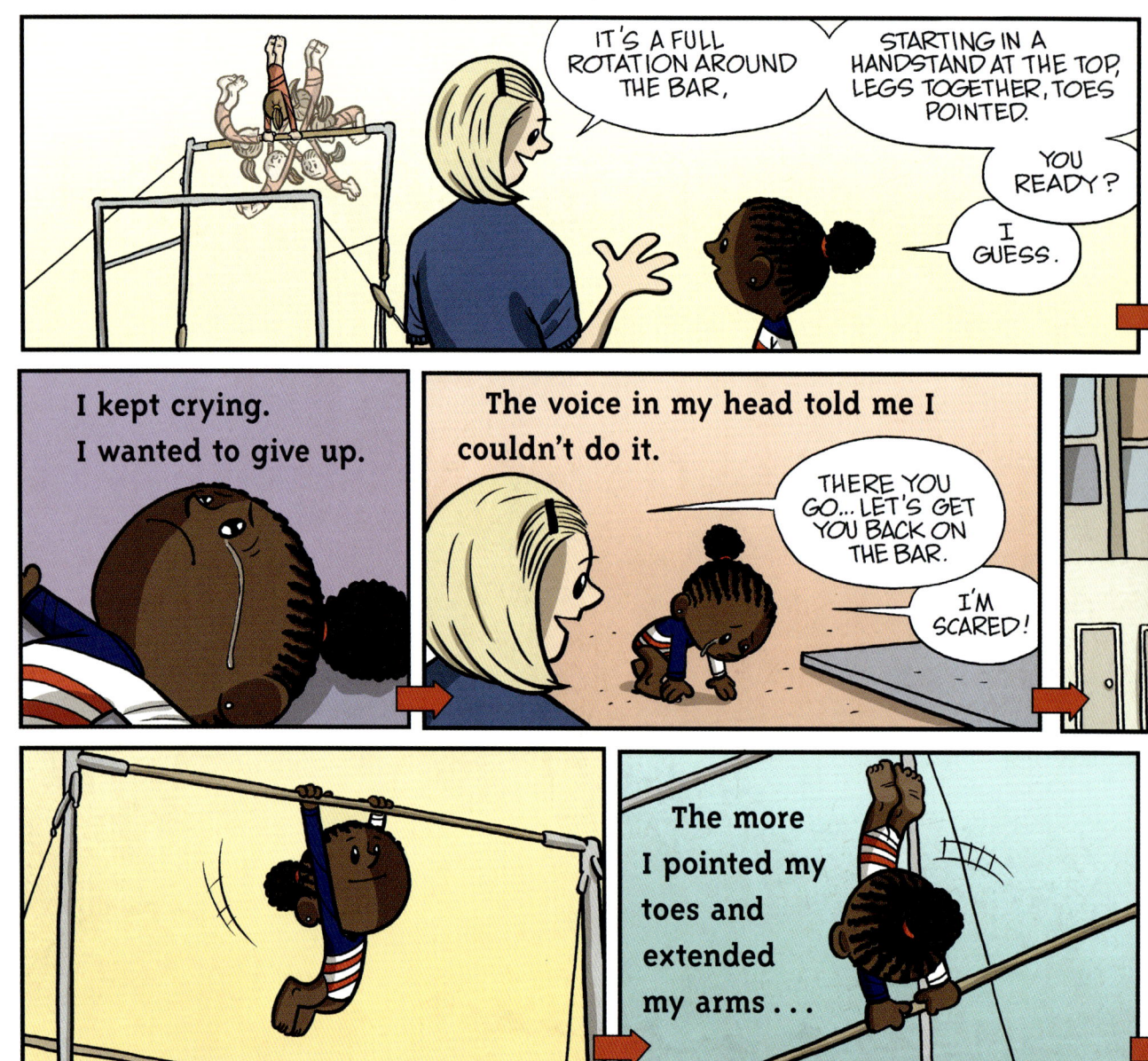

Usually, if you mess up, you fall into the foam pit. This time, I bounced off the bar, rolled down the steel cables, and crashed hard on the concrete.

I'M NEVER DOING THAT AGAIN.

But the more times I tried . . .

YOU GOT IT, SIMONE.

The more I focused on my form . . .

JUST LIKE THAT.

The more the negative voices in my head—my fear and anxiety—went quiet.

GREAT JOB.

YOU DID IT, SIMONE.

Being a top competitor takes physical health, which means a strong body. But it also takes great mental health, which means feeling emotionally strong.

> TO PUT IT SIMPLY, TO BE YOUR BEST,

> YOU NEED TO FEEL GOOD ABOUT YOURSELF.

In addition to anxiety, at nine years old, I was diagnosed with ADHD, Attention Deficit Hyperactivity Disorder.

That means it's hard for me to concentrate and sit still.

> MY BRAIN MOVES REALLY FAST, BUT SO DOES MY BODY,

> WHICH IS WHAT MAKES ME A GREAT GYMNAST.

> ADHD IS MY CHALLENGE **AND** MY SUPERPOWER.

You should never be ashamed to talk about your mental health.

At eleven years old, I decided I wanted to compete in the Olympics. To get there, I needed a lot of help.

There were coaches who were good for me . . .

SIMONE, GO OUT THERE AND ENJOY YOURSELF.

THAT'S ALL THAT MATTERS.

Coaches who were intense with me . . .

YOU NEED TO STOP FALLING ON THAT BEAM.

FOCUS.

MARTHA KÁROLYI

And one coach who was very bad for me.

To help me after a particularly rough performance, my parents had me meet regularly with a sports psychologist.

It was the final bit of help I needed.
A few weeks later, I became the 2013 U.S. National All-Around Champion.
Then I got selected for the U.S. World Championship team.
And then . . .

There was no stopping me.

This was my first Olympics. I was nineteen.
As always, I looked to the crowd to find my mom.

Critics said I was old to be a gymnast.
You think I let that stop me?

At the Olympics in Rio de Janeiro, I won four gold medals—Best All-Around, Best Floor Exercise, Best Vault, and Team Gold—plus a bronze for the Balance Beam.

In the closing ceremonies, they even asked me to carry the American flag!

Four years later, at the 2020 Olympics in Tokyo, people expected me to repeat it all—as if everything was the same.

But it wasn't.

Because of the COVID-19 pandemic, it was the first time my parents weren't in the stands. No one was.

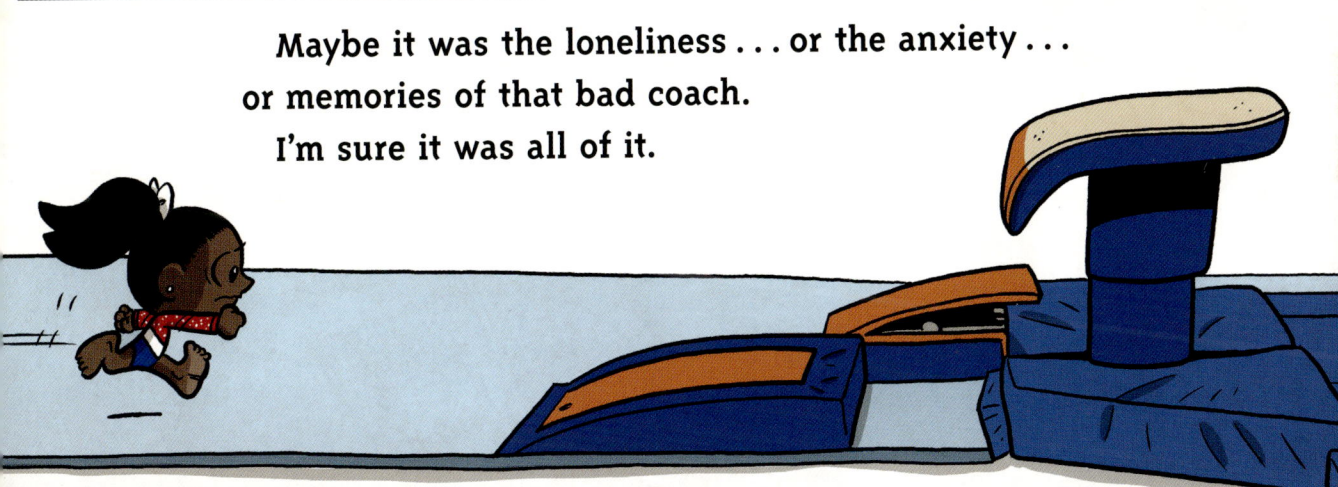

YOUR MOM'S WATCHING FROM HOME.

YOU GOT THIS, SIMONE.

Maybe it was the loneliness . . . or the anxiety . . . or memories of that bad coach.

I'm sure it was all of it.

Pushing off the vault, I got what's known as the twisties.
I couldn't "feel" where I was when I was spinning in the air.
I didn't know when to bring my feet down.

It was more than a shock. It was terrifying.
If I'd landed wrong, I could've been hurt . . . or even died.

Right there, I withdrew from the rest of the Olympic games.
I called my mom, who said she loved me.
But when it came to the public's reaction . . .

It was a disaster.

Was it a hard decision to withdraw? Of course.
Was it the right decision? Absolutely. I needed to take care of myself.
But now I wondered: Was this how my career was going to end?

Nearly two years later, I went back to the gym.
To start, I just jumped on the trampoline.

Even after winning so many gold medals, I was still nervous.
I wanted to quit so many times.

For strength, I relied on my family, my teammates, my three dogs. And of course, my therapist.

At the 2024 Olympics in Paris, at twenty-seven years old, I was the oldest woman to compete for American gymnastics since 1952.

This time, my parents were in the stands again.

I'm sure haters were there too.

Want to know the best thing about haters? Proving them wrong! Running full speed and dressed in fire-engine red, I let the world go quiet . . .

and did what I do best . . .

In my life, they called me a quitter.
A loser.
They even called me weak.
But there's nothing weak about admitting you don't have it all together.
In fact, it takes strength to ask for help and put your own well-being over the expectations of others.

We all have times when we feel scared and anxious.
We can't get rid of those feelings—they're part of what makes us human.
Next time you feel that way,
close your eyes,
take a deep breath,
and remember . . .

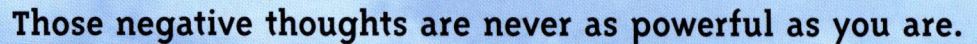

In sports, as in life, to reach the highest level, you need hard work, determination, and the ability to overcome your fears.

Will there be challenges along the way?

Absolutely.

Yet, as someone dear to me once said, "You grow through what you go through."

Find what makes you happy.
Find what makes you feel powerful.
Rise above the doubters, and prove them wrong.
You only fail if you stop trying.

I am Simone Biles.
Strong mind.
Strong body.
Strong you.

"You will not always be strong,
but you can always be brave."
–Simone Biles

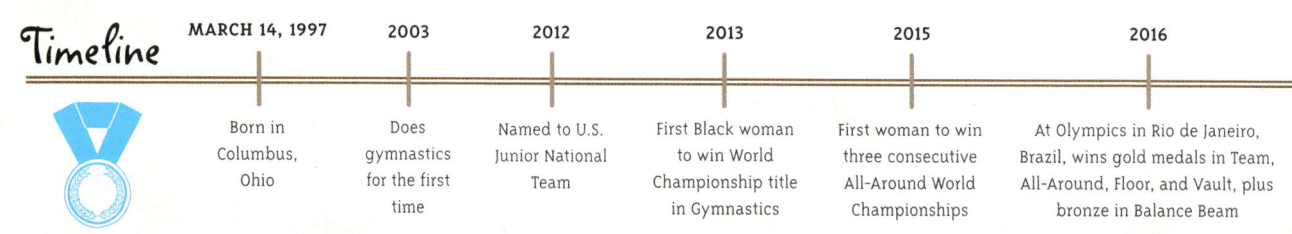

Simone with her parents in 2016

2024 Olympic medals

Competing in the 2024 Olympics

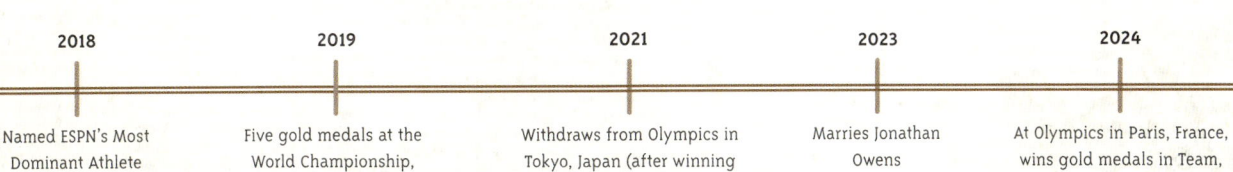

2018	2019	2021	2023	2024
Named ESPN's Most Dominant Athlete	Five gold medals at the World Championship, first to do it since 1958	Withdraws from Olympics in Tokyo, Japan (after winning silver medal in Team and bronze in Balance Beam)	Marries Jonathan Owens	At Olympics in Paris, France, wins gold medals in Team, All-Around, and Vault, plus silver in Floor

For my sister-in-law,
Ami Kuttler,
who knows what it takes,
mentally and physically
—B.M.

For Jeremy
Every day I'm impressed by your ability to prioritize
your mental health and those of your patients.
You're changing the world!
—C.E.

For historical accuracy, we used Simone Biles's actual words whenever possible.
For more of her true voice, we recommend and acknowledge the below works.

· ·

SOURCES

Courage to Soar: A Body in Motion, A Life in Balance by Simone Biles and Michelle Burford (Zondervan, 2016)

"Simone Biles on Overcoming Abuse, the Postponed Olympics, and Training During a Pandemic" by Abby Aguirre (*Vogue*, July 9, 2020)

"'I Should Have Quit Way Before Tokyo': For Simone Biles, walking away was an act of self-reclamation" by Camonghne Felix
(*New York* magazine, September 27, 2021)

"Forever Simone" by Leah Faye Cooper (*Vanity Fair*, February 2024)

Simone Biles Rising docu-series directed by Katie Walsh (Netflix, 2024)

FURTHER READING FOR KIDS

What Are the Summer Olympics? by Gail Herman (Penguin Workshop, 2016)

My Book of Gymnastics by Vincent Walduck (Dorling Kindersley, 2020)

She Persisted in Sports by Chelsea Clinton (Philomel, 2020)

· ·

ROCKY POND BOOKS
An imprint of Penguin Random House LLC, 1745 Broadway, New York, NY 10019

First published in the United States of America by Rocky Pond Books, an imprint of Penguin Random House LLC, 2025

Text copyright © 2025 by Forty-four Steps, Inc.
Illustrations copyright © 2025 by Christopher Eliopoulos

Colored by Jason Henry with Christopher Eliopoulos

Visit us online at penguinrandomhouse.com.
Library of Congress Cataloging-in-Publication Data is available.

Photo of Simone on page 38 by Ezra Shaw/Getty Images; photo of Simone with her parents by Melissa Phillip/Houston Chronicle/Hearst Newspapers via Getty Images; photo of Simone on the balance beam by Stefan Matzke—sampics/Getty Images; and photo of Simone with Olympic medals by Naomi Baker/Getty Images

Manufactured in China · ISBN 9780593533482
1 3 5 7 9 10 8 6 4 2

TOPL
Design by Jason Henry · Text set in Triplex

The illustrator created the artwork for this book using Wacom Cintiq and Clip Studio Paint with custom pencils and brushes.

The authorized representative in the EU for product safety and compliance is Penguin Random House Ireland, Morrison Chambers, 32 Nassau Street, Dublin D02 YH68, Ireland, https://eu-contact.penguin.ie.